The old Jail

Deakin's Cottage

St Patrick's

Exhibition Building

Parliament House

Fitzroy Gardens

Capt. Cook's Cottage

Bourke + Wills

Melbourne Club

Flinders St. Station

The Treasury

St Pauls

Princess Theatre

RIVER

St Kilda Road.

Shrine of rememberence

Government House.

La Trobe Cottage

MELBOURNE SKETCHBOOK

Further books in this series

MELBOURNE
SKETCHBOOK

text by
W. H. NEWNHAM

drawings by
UNK WHITE

RIGBY LIMITED

RIGBY LIMITED, JAMES PLACE, ADELAIDE
SYDNEY, MELBOURNE, BRISBANE, PERTH

First published 1967
Copyright 1967 by Bill Newnham and Unk White
Library of Congress Catalog Card Number 66-29795

Printed in Australia by Halstead Press Pty Ltd
for Rigby Limited, Adelaide.
Registered in Australia for transmission
by post as a book

CONTENTS

CUSTOMS HOUSE

The Customs House stands on Melbourne's most historic site, opposite the fresh water of the Yarra River which dictated the site of the future capital of Victoria. A small ironstone tablet let into the pavement at the William Street corner carries John Batman's oft quoted phrase 'This will be the place for a village.'

Unfortunately Batman's map shows the suggested site of the city at Fisherman's Bend, Port Melbourne, and his diary entry written some days after the discovery of the Yarra on 8 June 1835 reads 'the boat went up the large river I have spoken of . . . and I am glad to state, about six miles up the river, all good water and very deep. This will be the place for a village.'

Obviously it is very doubtful whether Batman himself went up the river. He left no party on the site which remained uninhabited until 29 August 1835 when John Pascoe Fawkner's party of freemen founded the city. Fawkner, a fellow Taswegian, who had become too seasick to continue with his partners, arrived on 11 October.

'The good water and very deep' became the site for Queens Wharf, the city's most important anchorage. This in turn determined the site of the Customs House.

The first Customs House was commenced in 1839, but in 1856 newer and grander offices were planned. These took twenty years to complete. The compensation is a fine Regency inspired building with impressive bluestone fence and cobblestoned courtyard behind.

The first shipping entry in the Customs House records links the city's two best-known pioneers. It records the arrival of the 86-ton schooner *Gem* owned by Batman until 1838, when she was bought by John Pascoe Fawkner.

MELBOURNE CLUB

The young blades of the original Melbourne Club were as different from their dignified descendants as their first meeting place—the small and primitive Lamb Inn—was from the Melbourne Club at 38 Collins Street, an elegant stone building in the best traditions of the London clubs then being designed by Sir Charles Barry.

At a lively dinner held on 1 January 1839 twenty-three officers and smart young men about town paid £2 each to found a club which hired a few rooms at the Lamb Inn, one of Melbourne's earliest hotels licensed in 1837. The Club later shifted to the corner of Market and Collins Streets. Finally, in 1858, the Club settled back to enjoy the measured calm and beauty of Collins Street East, in a building whose graceful Italian Renaissance façade is matched by a fine pair of old fashioned cast-iron light standards with tapered glass lanterns.

The favourite pastimes of the earliest members appear to have been souveniring door knockers, trade signs, toppers and actresses, ringing the fire bell suspended from a gum tree, tipping representatives of law and order into Lake Cashmore—a large muddy hole at the corner of Collins and Elizabeth Streets—and even attempting to tip over the tiny Pavilion Theatre.

With the arrival of numbers of eligible young ladies, the high-spirited members married. Their wives saw to it that they were transformed into solid citizens who tended to forget the time when their club kept a special annexe where members could sleep off a hectic evening or lie low for a while; where 'beer in the pewter and brandy neat or infused in cold and hot water and sugar' were always available with steaming hot dishes.

PARLIAMENT HOUSE

Parliament House, one of the handsomest classical buildings in Australia with its colonnade of nine Doric columns reached by an imposing flight of bluestone steps more than 140 feet wide, dominates the eastern end of busy Bourke Street. But it is still unfinished after 110 years—one reason for describing Melbourne as a 'city of unfinished palaces' and a reminder of the impatience of pioneer planners.

Building began in early 1856, and, despite workers striking for an eight-hour day, the Assembly and Legislative Council chambers were far enough advanced to be opened on 25 November by a son of the more famous John Macarthur, Sir Edward Macarthur, the acting Governor.

The handsome library, added in 1860, contains files of Parliamentary debates and some 150,000 books, many of them of great historical value. The large, richly carpeted central room looks out on impeccable lawns, tennis courts, a cricket pitch and bowling green. The vestibule and Queen's Hall were completed in 1879 and the façade was faced in 1892 with attractive Stawell freestone; but Parliament House still lacks the north and south wing and the 150 foot high dome planned by its architect, Peter Kerr.

Until 1851, Victoria (Port Phillip district) formed part of the colony of New South Wales, but when self-government was granted, the first Legislative Council sat in St Patrick's Hall in Bourke Street. The second home, after responsible government was introduced with two houses on the British pattern, was Parliament House, but in 1901, when Australia became a nation, State government was moved to the Exhibition and Federal Parliament took over the building.

In 1926, Federal Parliament moved to Canberra and State Parliament returned to its rightful home.

FIRST GOVERNMENT HOUSE

Victoria's first Government House, a prefabricated cottage shipped from England by La Trobe in 1839, sat on a small rise supposedly named Jolimont because his Swiss wife is said to have exclaimed "Quel joli mont!" on seeing it first. In fact, it reminded her of a beautiful hill overlooking her family's summer residence in Switzerland.

Ultimately, the cottage was swallowed up in a maze of buildings and factories, and its historical significance was almost lost. It became part of the grounds of a shoe manufacturing firm, Bedggood and Co., whose owners, on discovering the importance of the dilapidated building, restored it with an attractive garden. In 1964, the National Trust moved it to its present location.

The cottage might have disappeared much earlier when Governor Gipps directed that the land on which it stood should be publicly auctioned. When La Trobe protested, Gipps suggested that the land be made official property and that La Trobe be re-imbursed for the cost of the house. This alternative was not accepted and the land was auctioned but the sympathetic Melbournites refused to bid against La Trobe who got his 12½ acres for the upset price of £250.

La Trobe was reputed to have made a fortune of £40,000 when the land was later sub-divided, but this has always been strenuously denied by his descendants who point out that he was granted a pension by the British Government in 1864. Even were the story true, few would have begrudged La Trobe his good fortune. He was never given any official residence, he was never granted the full title of Governor, only Lt.-Governor, and his salary was never more than £2,000 a year whereas his immediate successor, Sir Charles Hotham, enjoyed the handsome sum of £15,000.

YOUNG AND JACKSON'S HOTEL

Very few people in Melbourne could direct you to the city's most famous hotel by its correct name because the Princes' Bridge Hotel is known simply as Young and Jackson's.

Originally, the block on which the hotel stands was bought by John Batman for £100 at the second land sales in 1837. Batman erected a small cottage used by Mrs E. Cooke for one of the first girls' schools. Later, in 1854, a three-storied bluestone building was erected for a local butcher and not until seven years later, was it given a licence as an hotel.

One of the best-known owners was James Mooney who kept the famous Royal at St Kilda which successfully withstood a siege by bushrangers in 1852. Later, Mooney sold out to two young gold diggers who had been successful in New Zealand—Mr Young and Mr Jackson.

Young and Jackson thought up a number of stunts to attract patrons, but none was more successful than the purchase of the famous nude painting Chloe, the work of Chevalier Jules le Febvre for whom she won a Grand Medal of Honor at the Paris Salon in 1876. She was awarded another gold medal at Melbourne's International Exhibition in 1882 but when she was exhibited a year later at the National Gallery on a Sunday afternoon, she caused a rare furore. The trustees were abused in the local press and Chloe was returned to her owner, an eminent surgeon, Sir Thomas FitzGerald. On his death in 1908, Chloe was bought by the shrewd young publicans whose customers suffered none of the inhibitions of the more puritanical citizens of the town.

Ultimately, she became quite respectable when she was exhibited by the Red Cross during the First World War and raised £300 for the comfort of soldiers.

GOVERNMENT HOUSE

In the 'sixties, Parliament decided that a new and more elaborate Government House was required but stated that it should not cost more than £25,000. The startled tenderers, on reading the specifications, were convinced it would. In addition to drawing, dining and waiting rooms, a ballroom 70 by 100 feet, twenty bedrooms, a shawl room and a library, the 'impressive edifice' was to be built in brick, rendered in Portland cement.

By the time Government House was completed in 1876 to the design of W. W. Wardell, the architect of St Patrick's Cathedral, the cost in the best of Australian large building traditions had risen to £154,000. It is, however, Melbourne's stateliest home, the centre of which is the lovely ballroom with its arcade and delightful musicians' gallery.

Built in bluestone in the Italianate style and modelled on Queen Victoria's Osborne House, the ivory-coloured stucco façade is impressive with Ionic columns above the Doric of the porticos below.

Everyone seemed pleased with the result except the first resident Governor, Sir George Bowen, who protested to the British Secretary of State that 'the Governor of Victoria is now called upon to maintain a Government House much larger than the official residence of the Lord Lieutenant of Ireland or the Viceroy of India, on less than half the salary and allowances of the first and one third . . . of the second.'

The gardens, seen at their best from the 145-foot tower, were once the home of aborigines whose primitive dances and tribal fights were seen by the earliest pioneers. More recently, in 1954, history repeated itself when 2,000 of Victoria's leading citizens struggled to see their Royal visitors at a Royal Garden party.

B

ST JAMES' OLD CATHEDRAL

Little has changed in St James' Old Cathedral since 2 October 1842 when an excited and well-dressed congregation proudly entered their new stone church. Here are the original box pews and cedar panelling, the canon's stall in the chancel, and the pews in the gallery where members of the 40th Regiment sat after they had escorted the Administrator, Mr La Trobe, to church. He sat with his family in one of the two private boxes high in the side walls which now house the organ pipes.

Here too is the original baptismal font from the Collegiate Church of Saint Katherine, London, a gift from Queen Victoria, in which Governor La Trobe's only son, Charles Joseph was baptized. Many other treasures remain, including a solid silver communion set dated 1848, the year in which Bishop Perry was enthroned and St James' became the Cathedral church of the new diocese of Melbourne.

In 1891, St James' became the Old Cathedral when St Paul's Cathedral was opened. With the loss of its title and the movement of people away from this part of the city, congregations gradually dwindled.

The church was moved in 1914 from the corner of William and Little Collins Streets to its present site near Flagstaff Gardens, where it was re-erected stone by stone.

One day a year, St James' recaptures some of its past glory when the annual Pioneers Service is held on the first Sunday in November. The historic church is packed with important vice-regal and civic guests, as well as the descendants of Robert Russell the architect; Rev. John C. Grylls the first minister; George Worcester the first choirmaster, and worshippers whose families have attended the small church for four or five generations.

MITRE TAVERN

The Mitre Tavern, resembling a typical English inn with its high gabled roof, tiny windows, but alas now minus its hitching post, is tucked away in Bank Place between William and Queen Streets, and remains the one reassuring survivor of the many hotels that once graced this part of Melbourne.

Scotts Hotel, originally the Lamb Inn, disappeared in comparatively recent years, long after Fawkner's Hotel opposite, as well as the Imperial Hotel made famous by the notorious Lola Montez and the Royal Hotel where Melbourne's first councillors elected their first mayor.

In the same area was Phairs Hotel and much earlier, the Angel Inn at the corner of Queen and Collins Streets, licensed with the second group of Melbourne hotels in 1837. The Angel boasted the city's first billiard room and was run by an extraordinary character, Edward Umphleby who quickly sickened of society and let his hotel for £250 a year to Thomas Halfpenny who renamed it the William Tell. In turn it was taken over, as were most of the other hotels, by a bank, the E.S. & A., and replaced by a charming Venetian Gothic building, suggesting the peace of a cathedral.

The Mitre, erected in the days when Victoria provided one hotel to every 294 people, compared to one to 2,079 in 1965, has never been a quiet place. It has always been the home of clubs and informal gatherings where artists, lawyers and writers have gathered regularly to engage in wordy battles on the site of a very old 'house,' the Waterloo, built by John Bullivant, a survivor of that battle. Bullivant was succeeded by a vivacious widow whose husband, a teetotaller, wrote an anthem called 'Will the Coming Man Drink Wine?' the answer to which has been exultantly given for the past one hundred years.

ST PAUL'S CATHEDRAL

Bishop Goe at the opening of St Paul's Cathedral struck the great door thrice with his pastoral staff and declaimed 'Open ye the gates.' Unfortunately 'the gates' remained closed and it was only when the knock was repeated with some force that the door swung back for his singularly necessary but traditional words 'Peace be to this house.'

Since then St Paul's has provided a quiet corner in a busy part of the city. Opposite stand two noisy railway stations and an equally animated hotel, Young and Jackson's, whose proprietors once rolled the beer barrels into the cathedral when the hotel was threatened by fire.

In the earliest days, Dr Alexander Thompson, catechist of the Port Phillip Association, read services in a tent pitched on this site that was later to become a hay and corn market. The land was finally granted to Bishop Perry who opened his parish church of St Paul in 1852.

Bishop Perry had always dreamed of a cathedral to replace St James' but his appeal for funds was not successful. Even the energetic and forceful Bishop Moorhouse despaired until an anonymous donor, a Presbyterian, Francis Ormond, gave the necessary £5,000 to commence building.

Finally in 1891, the year that Perry died, the Cathedral built to the design of William Butterfield, one of England's great church architects, was consecrated, but the tower and spires were not added for another forty years. With its central spire 314 feet high, the second highest Anglican spire in the world, St Paul's stands not only as a fine example of post-Gothic revivalist architecture but as a memorial to Bishop Perry who never saw the cathedral which, in turn, never saw its architect who supervised the first part of its construction from England.

THE ROYAL MINT

On 17 November 1838, three years after the foundation of Melbourne, the majority of the 2,000 inhabitants turned out to see the city's first cricket match in which the newly formed Melbourne Club defeated a team from the military in a game played with 'an esprit de corps, judgement and activity that a first rate club in England might not be ashamed of.' An old account book shows that only £2.3.0 was spent on the necessary two bats, balls and stumps.

By 1931, the Royal Mint on the same site had coined more than 147,000,000 sovereigns and nearly 2,000,000 half sovereigns. For the past two and a half years, the Mint has been turning out an astronomical number of decimal currency copper coins, 3,000,000 one cent pieces every week.

A square stone building still stands opposite the Royal Mint on the north-west corner of William and Little Lonsdale Streets, looking much the same as a hundred years ago when it also dealt with millions of pounds in raw gold. The building is depicted in an old engraving entitled 'Arrival of the Gold Escort 1852.'

Melbourne's first exhibition was staged on the site of the Royal Mint in 1854, and a commemorative medal shows a large wood and iron building—275 by 90 feet—with fluted columns and impressive façade.

However, it cannot be compared with the present palatial Royal Mint completed in 1872, set behind an iron railing fence with carriage gates at either end emblazoned with the Royal Arms in colour, and guarded by small lodges flanked by magnificent oleanders. It must be satisfying to the Public Works office that the Royal Mint, designed by its own architects, is a treasure in itself, being classified as 'A' by the National Trust of Victoria.

ST PATRICK'S CATHEDRAL

St Patrick's Cathedral took eighty years to grow into what is now regarded as one of the finest examples in Australia of the Gothic Revival style. Even purists who argue that the 340 foot spire—90 feet higher than that planned by the designer—is out of proportion, will readily admit the handsome proportions of the interior, the long and impressive vista of the nave, and the sensitive treatment of the arches.

Against the wishes of the City Council Governor La Trobe approved a grant of five acres on which a small wooden church was first built. This was followed by the foundation on 9 April 1850 of St Patrick's church, although work was later suspended when workmen vanished to the goldfields. By the time labour became available again the church was considered too small for the growing congregation. It was pulled down, and by early 1858 the first section of a new church was so far advanced that Pontifical Mass was celebrated on 14 February. Before this year was out however, a cathedral was planned and the third church disappeared.

St Patrick's Cathedral, designed by William Wardell, was opened in November 1868. The erection of the massive central tower began in 1870, followed by the extension of the nave and aisles, and the addition of transepts and chapels. Even so, when Bishop Goold died in 1886, the great church was still unfinished. His successor Archbishop Thomas Joseph Carr was determined to complete the cathedral, and in 1897 St Patrick's was consecrated with additional sanctuaries, sacristies and cloisters. But it remained for Archbishop Mannix to add the finishing touches of the three spires.

The three spires tower above the remains of the early small church which, because of lack of funds, were incorporated into the walls of St Patrick's Cathedral.

PRINCESS THEATRE

The Princess Theatre, with its flamboyant façade of allegorical figures and three huge Imperial crowns surmounting an irreverent angel blowing its own trumpet, has the longest association with show business of any theatre in Melbourne.

It began as Astley's Amphitheatre in 1854 when the lush and extravagant days of the gold boom gave Melbourne more 'live' and varied theatre than it has enjoyed before or since. With the theatres Royal, Olympic, and Queen's, it provided for more than 8,000 patrons regularly every night. In addition, the notorious Salle de Valentino, the new Exhibition building, and Cremorne Gardens beckoned to thousands of other free spenders.

The recession in the mid-'fifties hit all entertainments and it appeared certain that Astley's would be sold. Happily George Selth Coppin, 'the father of the Australian theatre', confidently took it over, redecorated it, lit it with gas and re-opened it on 18 February 1856 with an expensive production featuring the then famous Bacchus Minstrels.

Later, even with colourful artists like Lola Montez, the theatre had many anxious moments, but it was still very much alive in 1887 when, for Queen Victoria's Jubilee, it was renamed and rebuilt to the design of one of Melbourne's most successful architects with an equally famous name, William Pitt. William, in addition to giving to the theatre an unrestrained and jolly type of architectural mayhem, evidenced in the Rialto, Olderfleet and Federal hotels, added a sliding ceiling to be rolled back on warm nights.

In the eighty years since then, the Princess has glittered with glamorous occasions, though for a while it became a film studio for the late F. W. Thring and later a cinema. Today it remains one of Melbourne's few legitimate theatres.

FIRE BRIGADE HEADQUARTERS

Nothing will draw a crowd more quickly than a large city fire. When to this excitement is added the fierce rivalry between the city's first fire brigade members, high entertainment is guaranteed.

Fire was an ever present hazard in early Melbourne with its many wooden houses, and the first insurance companies, seriously affected by disastrous fires, formed their own brigades, offering their men 20/- attendance bonus money but fining them 10/- for absence. Each insurance company affixed its individual firemark or steel plate to the insured buildings, and it was not uncommon for the brigade chief to inspect the plaque first. If it belonged to a rival company, his men retreated—not always gracefully.

On the other hand, members of suburban Council brigades formed in the 'fifties made superhuman efforts to claim 'first water' bonuses, often dragging their carts miles to make money and headlines. Civic pride rode high. Local councils dressed their men in brilliant uniforms, and great crowds turned out for their displays and torchlight processions. However, many citizens complained when firemen held off members of other brigades to protect their bonuses, and when exuberant fights followed.

Even so, some councils were opposed to consolidation until 1883 when the old Bijou Theatre in Bourke Street was burnt down and two firemen lost their lives. The subsequent inquiry recommended amalgamation, and in 1893 the Metropolitan Fire Brigade was founded.

From the tall tower of its headquarters at Eastern Hill, the lookout men once found it easy to detect the glow of a dangerous fire in any part of the city. Today more modern methods are used.

ST FRANCIS' MONASTERY

The earliest settlers prided themselves on religious toleration. Melbourne's first small wooden church was used by several denominations and appeals for church buildings were made to all citizens irrespective of their beliefs. So the small community was shocked when it was discovered the day after the foundation of St Francis' Catholic Church on 4 October 1841 that the stone had been moved and all the coins, worth a mere 30/-, stolen.

In the first census, in October 1836, only 14 of the population of 224 were recorded as Catholics. This group met on the present site of the Olderfleet in Collins Street, at the home of a 'pious French carpenter' Peter Bodecin, but by 1839 they were asking for contributions from 'Protestant and Christian brethren' to build a church. That year, Father Patrick Bonaventure Geoghegan arrived, and the first Mass was celebrated in the unroofed store of Hogue and Campbell at the north-east corner of Elizabeth and Little Collins Streets.

Designed by Samuel Jackson in the Romantic Gothic style, St Francis' possesses clean and simple lines with graceful pinnacles to relieve the single buttresses. Its outward appearance is almost the same as it was a century ago, but one unpopular change was the cutting down of an old gum tree in the 1920s. A compromise was reached when it was agreed that the wood should be used for three episcopal chairs, now in St Patrick's Cathedral. Another change was St Francis' transfer, in 1929, to the Fathers of the Blessed Sacrament.

But the greatest change is from the small congregation when the church was considered 'out in the bush' to the more than 10,000 worshippers who now throng the church weekly.

C

MENZIES HOTEL

When Menzies Hotel opened in 1867, Sydney's Petty's Hotel lost its place as Australia's leading hotel. Designed by Melbourne architect, Joseph Reed, who designed among other buildings the Town Hall, the Library, the old Wilson Hall and many of the early churches of the city, and built by David Mitchell, father of Dame Nellie Melba, the great pile of plastered brickwork which cost £32,000, was rich in panelling, gas chandeliers, thick carpets and exotic dishes prepared by the chef Mr Bennet, newly arrived from the kitchens of Buckingham Palace.

Soon visitors were autographing a book that is now a collector's dream. The first British Royal visitor in 1861, the Duke of Edinburgh, was a frequent guest; Samuel Clemens, or Mark Twain, stoked the hotel's boilers when he was weight reducing; Anthony Trollope wrote 'I have never put myself up at a better inn in any part of the world' while Paderewski restored the balance when he claimed that the food was 'simply indescribable' and that he lived on pine-apples until his wife cooked meals in his room.

Built on a block of land bought for £67 in the first land sales of 1837, the hotel was first owned by Archibald Menzies who with his wife Catherine ran a little inn at 235 Lonsdale Street, which became popular with country families when Menzies, even in the gold crazy days, refused to raise the tariff beyond £3.12.6. Millions of pounds and tens of thousands of acres changed hands in the Commercial Room.

When Menzies moved, he asked the 'squatters of Victoria and the Riverina' to follow him. They have, ever since, despite the blandishments of more modern hotels. Fortunes still change hands, the waiters are still there in their Menzies tartan—but the charge is no longer £3.12.6 a week.

TREASURY BUILDING

One of the most interesting features of the Treasury building is seldom seen—a series of huge underground vaults which once held fortunes in gold guarded by smart, blue-uniformed soldiers. Another feature was a third floor flat provided for the Governor's aide-de-camp who enjoyed a coach house of his own and stabling amenities.

The vaults are still there, but the gold, soldiery and the Governor's aide have disappeared. However, the handsome building is little changed and stands as a reminder of the adolescence of a precocious city enjoying a £100,000,000 gold rush.

While the Treasury is today recognized as one of the most satisfying buildings in Melbourne, with its elegant arcaded Renaissance façade and deeply recessed offices with their own balconies, its graceful fluted columns and splendid fenestration, the plan was strongly criticized because 'it was so devoid of the graces of architecture.'

The contract for the stone facing of Bacchus Marsh freestone over brick and bluestone was awarded to a Mr Huckson for what today seems the absurdly small sum of £17,716. When the building was finished in 1862, it was greatly admired but the appearance of the impressive portico was completely spoiled by 'abominable wooden steps' which almost literally gave way to the present solid bluestone approach added in 1867.

When the Treasury was being built, many people complained that it was at the wrong end of town. But the removal of the Treasury office from the western end at least exonerated its first clerk, honest Mr McVittie, who had been accused of stealing gold, was acquitted, but lost his job. The missing packet was found in a pigeon hole!

BURKE AND WILLS MONUMENT

This massive monument overlooking the northern end of Spring Street is a memorial to Australia's most ambitious expedition whose leaders, the flamboyant Irish police inspector Robert O'Hara Burke, and the quiet English scientist William John Wills, were the first to cross the Australian continent south to north.

No explorers left with higher hopes or better equipment, provided as they were with flat-bottomed boats to sail the expected inland sea and air bags to be tied under the jaws of camels as they swam wide rivers and lakes. The party led by Burke left the city to the cheers of thousands of holiday makers on 20 August 1860. Ten months later it was reduced to a pathetic and needless tragedy in the centre of Australia, at Cooper's Creek, with one forlorn survivor, John King.

The bodies of Burke and Wills were brought back to the city to lie in state for twenty days while more than 100,000 mourners filed past. On 21 January 1863 every building was subdued in purple and black as enormous crowds silently watched the mile and a half cortège go by with State leaders, clergy, soldiers and mutes paying their tribute. Guns saluted at minute intervals and the strains of the Dead March accompanied the rumbling of the great hearse.

The imposing memorial was sculpted by Charles Summers who not only modelled the huge figures and cast them in bronze but built the large furnace himself. The monument, towards which the government donated £5,000, was first erected at the corner of Collins and Russell Streets, but when cable trams were introduced in 1886, the statue was moved to Spring Street where it stands as a memorial to an extraordinary expedition which will always be remembered by Australians because it ended not in triumph, but in tragedy.

MELBOURNE BOYS' HIGH SCHOOL

Melbourne High and MacHigh, as MacRobertson Girls' High School is called, began as the Model School opened in 1854 in a handsome £45,000 building in Spring Street at a 'quit rent of a peppercorn yearly on demand.' Ironically, these schools are today the only two segregated high schools in the State.

In 1848, a Denominational School Board had been established to control church schools which were then receiving grants of £20,000 a year. Four years later, the Board of National Education was founded to organize State schools. The Model School was an attempt to show what the State could achieve.

The first headteachers, Mr and Mrs Arthur Davitt who were paid a joint salary of £1,000 a year, appear to have earned their money because, in less than three months, '705 pupils were scribbling with pens and paper from Ireland.' The school was co-educational, fees were 1/- to 2/- payable ten weeks in advance; parents and even friends were welcomed to inspect the classes.

Although boys and girls entered by separate gates and played in separate yards, the more daring girls including the famous Australian actress, Nellie Stewart, made school exciting by raiding the boys' playground.

Through the years the school's importance declined, but in 1905 it again became significant as Melbourne Continuation School, the first of many secondary schools. However, in the late 'twenties the boys were transferred to their new and imposing £100,000 building on Forrest Hill, South Yarra, while the girls moved to the temporary premises of Government House. Finally, the girls took over their present impressive premises, the gift of Sir Macpherson Robertson.

SCOTCH COLLEGE

In 1872, the Victorian Attorney-General, J. Stephen Wilberforce, a grandson of William Wilberforce, introduced a bill for 'a free, secular and compulsory system of education' and soon afterwards, Melbourne papers were trumpeting that 'Victoria leads the world in education for the people.'

In the year following, 453 common schools became the State schools of today and negotiations began for the purchase of 590 church schools. A number of church schools refused state control, forfeiting any rights to government assistance. Thus we still have our Public schools including the earliest, Scotch College, established by Melbourne's leading Presbyterian preacher and leader, James Forbes. The college began as Chalmer's Free Church School at 237 Spring Street, but after another two moves Scotch College settled down in Glenferrie Road, Hawthorn, on sixty acres of what was Victoria's first cattle run.

Scotch's first headmaster, William Lawson from Dunoon, Scotland, was followed by another two Scotsmen, unlike in many ways but both dedicated headmasters. Alexander Morrison was only twenty-eight when he took over in July 1857. His brother, Dr G. Morrison was headmaster of Geelong College. His nephew became known as 'Chinese' Morrison, the famous *Times* correspondent in Peking.

When Morrison died in 1903, William Still Littlejohn, the next headmaster, broadened the scope of the college giving it a reputation for outstanding success in both scholarship and sport. Back in 1858, on 7 August, although unofficial games had been played earlier, Scotch and the Church of England's Melbourne Grammar contested the first recorded game of Australian rules football, with goals more than a mile apart at Jolimont and Richmond. The forty men a side battled for three days to win the match.

COMO HOUSE

This loveliest of stately homes in Melbourne still retains a high proportion of original furniture including some made by a Richmond firm of undertakers who turned to this more congenial work during their slack periods. The ballroom, lit by a superb chandelier, is the most impressive room with its full-length windows topped by gold silk pelmets brought out from England in 1853. Here, every Friday night during the winter months, eighty elegantly dressed people enjoyed themselves on a floor made perfect by shredded wax candles and sprung on chains to make dancing easier.

Como House stands on land first settled by squatter David Hill; later the property of $54\frac{1}{2}$ acres passed to Captain William Lonsdale, first superintendent of the colony. After being held by Edward Eyre Williams who gave the estate its name and by John Brown who developed it, Como was sold to Charles Armytage in 1864. His family held it for the next ninety-five years. In 1959, by which time the grounds had been reduced to $5\frac{1}{2}$ acres, the keys of the property were handed over to the National Trust of Victoria by a great-great-grandson of Charles Henry Armytage.

It is not difficult to appreciate the planning of Como's grounds by Baron von Mueller, the Director of the Botanic Gardens, or to picture those occasions when cherry picking was an annual excitement or when the trees were hung with Japanese lanterns to welcome over 400 guests to gala balls.

Como attracts more than 50,000 visitors every year and rightly so for its setting effectively re-creates the atmosphere and mood of a home built in what was to become known in Melbourne as the Age of Elegance. The National Trust has already spent $293,000 on the property.

PETER PAN

Melbourne is noted for its many lovely parks and gardens but not for its squares and statues. It has none of the former and comparatively few worthwhile examples of the latter. The odd thing is that so many of these few are the work of one man, Paul Montford, who came to Melbourne in 1923 but found it difficult to make a living although he had been one of the most brilliant students of the Royal Academy in London. Fortunately, many years of work followed his winning designs for sculpture on the Shrine of Remembrance.

One of his finest small bronzes is Peter Pan which once graced the Alexandra Gardens and was donated by Alderman Jeffries. Equally delightful works are the Water Nymph in the Queen Victoria Gardens and The Court Favourite in Flagstaff Gardens. So too is Montford's statue of Adam Lindsay Gordon, in Carpentaria Place which depicts the poet lounging comfortably in riding clothes, book in hand with an arm negligently flung over the back of the chair. For this work Montford was awarded in 1934 the gold medal of the Royal Society of British Sculptors for the best piece of sculpture for that year.

Opposite, near the Treasury, sits his George Higinbotham, one of the outstanding Chief Justices of Victoria, though this work is not as successful as the statue of Charles Wesley which dominates the front of Wesley Church. The impressive *bas* reliefs of eight Australian statesmen in King's Hall, Canberra, and his war memorial for the Australian Club, Sydney, all underline Montford's versatility if indifference to the ideas of the modern school of sculpture.

It seems fitting therefore that his romantic Peter Pan, withdrawn from the Alexandra Gardens because of vandalism will soon sit happily in Melbourne's first Civic Square near the Melbourne Town Hall.

GENERAL POST OFFICE

The first letters to Melbourne were carried by obliging sea captains who left them at John Batman's house, but the first official postmaster was Captain Benjamin Baxter, Clerk of the Bench, whose wife did most of the postal work in a cottage on swampy ground near the corner of King Street and Flinders Lane. Two months after making up the first mail to England, in January 1839, Mrs Baxter and her children were rescued by boat when floodwaters of the Yarra almost washed the small post office away.

After several changes, the Post Office opened for business at its present location on 11 April 1841 with a title which gave it the right to sink wells for 'domestic, agricultural, farming and irrigation purposes'—a title which suggests a government humorist because Elizabeth Street often became a raging torrent and the ground was so soggy that only two storeys were erected in eight years. The final floor and clock tower were added in 1889, giving the building the doubtful distinction of three types of architecture—Doric on the ground, Ionic on the second, and Corinthian on the third floor.

Although the Post Office is a busy and animated centre today, it lacks the colour of the gold-rush era when miners queued for letters, when Cobb and Co. coaches stood by waiting for the country mail, and scribes in small booths wrote letters for customers anxious to catch the London mail. The telegraph messengers on horseback, the departmental heads in black silken toppers and frock coats and the P.M.G. band in gay uniforms have also disappeared. But so too have the Elizabeth Street floods which were so bad that Captain McMillan, who served under Nelson, suggested that the street should be turned into a canal.

D

CAPTAIN COOK'S COTTAGE

This small stone cottage set in Fitzroy Gardens is a memorial to one of the world's greatest navigators. Born the second son of a farm labourer in Marston, Yorkshire, on 27 October 1728, Cook was twenty-seven years old before he joined the Royal Navy. Yet a mere twenty-four years later, he was famous for his voyages of discovery which had taken him around the world, and made him an honoured member of the Royal Society.

It is a pity then that the house has to be labelled 'this building is known as Captain Cook's cottage.' Although Cook never lived in it, it did belong to his parents at Great Ayton; their initials above the lintel, J. C. and G., standing for James and Grace. Moreover Cook certainly visited the cottage after he returned from his first great journey when he discovered Australia in 1770.

This began in 1768 when he led a Royal Society expedition to the South Pacific to observe the transit of Venus. He also carried secret instructions to search for a southern continent and 'take possession . . . in the name of the King of Great Britain.' After he had sighted Venus at Tahiti, Cook sailed up the eastern coast of Australia, naming Botany Bay on 29 April 1770 and taking possession of the whole of the eastern part of the continent on 22 August.

The odd thing is that Cook might never have gone to sea. He was a grocer's boy when he came across an unusual shilling in the till for which he substituted his own. He was charged with theft but though he was proved innocent, he resented the accusation and almost immediately joined John Walker, a near-by coal shipping firm at Whitby—from which time his interest lay in the sea and ships.

VICTORIA MARKET

This lively sixteen-acre market, where more stallholders sell a greater variety of goods than anywhere else in Australia, was once the dreary site of Melbourne's first general cemetery which became so dilapidated that the public contributed £200 to erect a fence to keep out stray cattle, and rogues who stole the solid red-gum headstones for firewood.

Although the first graveyard was on Flagstaff Hill, ten acres were set aside in the city's first survey for a general cemetery. One of the first funerals was that of the young son of Melbourne's best-known minister, Adam Thomson, whose coffin was borne by six young women followed by many of the Sunday school children of the tiny settlement.

The cemetery was closed in 1853 but it was used intermittently until 1917, when it was estimated that more than 10,000 people had been buried there. The Victoria market, opened in March 1878, was extended when the cemetery was finally moved in 1922.

Since then, it has been one of the busiest centres in the city. In addition to the retail market where stallholders pay 50c. for standings on Tuesdays and Thursdays and $1.30 on Fridays and Saturdays, the wholesale market buys the produce of market gardeners, orchardists and horticulturists at a mile and a half of standings costing $14.00 for three months. Buyers range from smartly dressed women and office workers to down and outs looking for free food.

The flower pavilion transforms drab surroundings into a fairyland of colour and perfume which should effectively drive away the ghosts of three bushrangers buried outside the main fence who were said to have once haunted the old cemetery.

UNIVERSITY OF MELBOURNE

Melbourne University was founded by a future Chancellor of the Exchequer, twenty-five year old Hugh Culling Eardley Childers who on 4 November 1852, as Auditor General and Finance Minister, proposed in his first speech in the Victorian Legislative Council, that £10,000 be allotted on the grounds that 'Sydney has a University and I would trust that before long, Melbourne might also be able to boast of one.'

In July 1854, the foundation stone was laid for a University on 100 acres of rough swampy land—anything but the first choice. Land near Parliament House was thought too valuable, and the Domain site with thousands of tent dwellers paying 5/- per tent, far too profitable. Childers had arranged that sixty acres be set aside for colleges to be endowed by wealthy benefactors but when no offers had been made by 1861, and the public was looking hungrily at the open spaces, ten acres each were granted to the Catholic, Presbyterian, Methodist and Anglican churches.

Even so, it was 1879 before Ormond (Presbyterian) was founded, ironically through the generosity of Francis Ormond, a well known Melbourne patron. Trinity (Anglican) had preceded Ormond in 1872; Queen's (Methodist) and Newman (Catholic) followed slowly in 1887 and 1916. With the addition of Janet Clarke Hall and Women's College in 1881 Melbourne became the first Australian university to admit women students.

Ormond's first master, Sir John Henry MacFarland, completed fifty-six years of unbroken association with the University when he ultimately held the post of Chancellor until his death in 1935. The first Chancellor, Sir Redmond Barry, the father of the University, died in 1880.

FLINDERS STREET RAILWAY
STATION

'I'll meet you under the clocks' still means only one place in Melbourne—the hand-operated clocks under the main entrance to Flinders Street railway station indicating the departure times of the hundreds of suburban trains which leave one of the world's largest terminals every day.

Before the small, squat railway station which stood at the end of Elizabeth Street was built, the land near by was a pleasant meadow used by anglers returning with fine catches of perch and bream from the Yarra.

In 1892, this was moved to make way for a 'giant railway terminus.' Plans were delayed with the bursting of the land boom, but by 1900 the 'respectable square building of yellow brick,' a fruit market, was pulled down to make way for the station in French Renaissance style. With three storeys Melbourne's largest building to that time was made more impressive with two clock towers, one a copper dome copied from St Paul's, London, and the other a square tower.

The first steam train in Australia departed from the smaller station on 12 September 1854. To the cheers of thousands, the Governor, Sir Charles Hotham and the vice-regal party entered first class carriages while grit and smoke enveloped the band of Her Majesty's 40th Regiment playing in an open truck at the back. The three miles to Port Melbourne took ten minutes—less time than it takes today. In fairness it should be added that the train now stops at several stations on the way, and it does not require, as it did on the first journey, the weight of many massive policemen urged on by the Governor to get the train moving on the return journey to the city.

MELBOURNE PUBLIC LIBRARY

When the first prince to visit Australia, the young French nobleman, the Duc de Prenthieve looked in at the Melbourne Library in 1866, he was astonished to see 'four hundred or more of the working class enjoying the amenities of a fine library.' He also noted that, even then, Melbourne's Sundays were dull.

The Library, whose foundation stone was laid on the same day as that of the University, 3 July 1854, began as a small fifty foot square room with 8,000 books, many of them unpacked and arranged by the energetic Sir Redmond Barry the first President of Trustees.

The north wing was completed in 1864 while the imposing portico with its fine Doric columns came six years later to give the Library its present appearance. The most impressive addition of many since then, was the massive octagonal reading room built in 1913, and measuring 115 feet in diameter with a ceiling 114 feet high covered by an 1,800-ton dome, the largest of its kind in the world at that time.

Millions of books pack the shelves and galleries with priceless treasures which range from the diaries of Batman and Fawkner, Melbourne's two great pioneers, and first folios of Captain Cook to practically every worthwhile book published each year in the English language.

Through the years, the Library has been joined by a splendid Gallery, Museum, Technological Museum and the La Trobe Library concentrating on Victoriana, to provide a group of buildings where it is possible to enjoy, almost under one roof, world famous paintings, valuable historical records, fine glass and technological wonders, as well as that most popular museum exhibit, the Australian wonder horse, Phar Lap.

FLEMINGTON RACECOURSE

It seems appropriate that Melbourne's first sheep were shorn opposite what is now Flemington racecourse. Four years later in 1840, racing was officially launched when the Port Phillip Turf Club was founded and the course was moved from the flat land between Spencer Street and North Melbourne railway stations to Flemington.

The first winning post was near the Maribyrnong River probably because so many racegoers travelled to the course by all kinds of river craft. By 1851, the *Maitland* was carrying 1,000 passengers at 2/6 a head, a charge that included the music of a nigger minstrel band and free salted herrings from large casks placed at strategic points along the deck, seemingly in anticipation of the many groggeries near the disembarkation point.

On 7 November 1861 the first Melbourne Cup was run for 'twenty sovereigns with another two hundred added,' and trains to the course from the city were introduced with fares at 1/6 first and 1/- second class.

Today, the Melbourne Cup is a national institution. Staid citizens who never bet on another race have a mild flutter, millions of dollars are wagered on the race, and work stops when the race is broadcast and telecast by the A.B.C. But the confident days of the gay 'nineties should not be forgotten when, in a city of 500,000, more than 100,000 attended the classic.

Ironically the greatest crowd of 200,000 had nothing to do with cheering on such champions of the turf as Carbine, Phar Lap, Comic Court or Galilee, but was at Flemington in 1934, to welcome two Englishmen, Scott and Black, who landed seventy-one hours after leaving London to win the Melbourne Centenary Air Race.

THE EXHIBITION BUILDING

Architects contemptuously described the Exhibition, as it is usually called, as a monstrosity of Italian and French styles and the public criticized it as a 'white elephant.' However, it has proved one of the most useful of all public buildings and one which avoided the worst excesses of the Corinthian period in Melbourne.

Although the first international exhibitions had been staged in 1854 on the site of the Royal Mint, and in the 'sixties and 'seventies in a new wooden building at the rear of the Public Library, the first really ambitious exhibition was planned in 1877. The foundation stone was laid in February 1879, and twenty months later the huge twenty-two acre building with a dome similar to Crystal Palace and higher than St Paul's, London, was welcoming the first of 1,330,000 visitors who thronged the exhibition in the next seven months.

In 1888, the centenary year of Australia, a second exhibition attracted two million people of whom more than half a million attended 244 concerts conducted by Sir Frederick Cowan. In the best traditions of all exhibitions, it cost the government almost ten times the estimated loss of £25,000.

Since its foundation the Exhibition has been used for every kind of entertainment and occasion, from that of an emergency hospital during the influenza epidemic of 1919 to the opening of the first Australian Parliament on 10 May 1901 by the Duke and Duchess of Cornwall and York.

The Exhibition may regain some of its initial importance if and when the next international exhibition is held in Melbourne, the first since 1890 when the cost so staggered the city fathers that they have apparently been frightened ever since.

Flemington Racecourse

St James's

Osmond College University

Fire Brigade Tower

The Mint

Post Office

The Library

Victoria Markets

Law Courts

St James Cathedral

Peter Pan

Menzie's Hotel

Young Jacks Hotel

The Mitre

Customs House

YARRA

N

W E

S